D0478699

J598.91 Julivert, Angels.
JUL   The fascinating
c.1   world of-- birds
$15.49   of prey
                    APR 15 1997

MAR 25 1998

DATE DUE

nov. 10			
GAYLORD			PRINTED IN U.S.A.

BIRDS OF PREY

CONTENTS

Original title of the book in Spanish:
El Fascinante Mundo de... Las Aves Rapaces
© Copyright Parramón Ediciones, S.A.
Published by Parramón Ediciones, S.A., Barcelona, Spain.

Author: Maria Ángels Julivert
Illustrations: Marcel Socías Studios

English text © Copyright 1996 by Barron's Educational
Series, Inc.

All rights reserved.
No part of this book may be reproduced in any form, by
photostat, microfilm, xerography, or any other means,
or incorporated into any information retrieval system,
electronic or mechanical, without the written permission of
the copyright owner.

All inquiries should be addressed to:
Barron's Educational Series, Inc.
250 Wireless Boulevard
Hauppauge, NY 11788-3917

ISBN: 0-8120-9424-7

Library of Congress Catalog Card No. 95-47343

Library of Congress Cataloging-in-Publication Data

Julivert, Maria Ángels.
  [Fascinante mundo de las aves rapaces. English]
  The fascinating world of —birds of prey / (text, Maria Ángels
Julivert; illustrations, Marcel Socías Studios).
      p.   cm.
  Includes index.
  Summary: Examines the breeding, eating, and living habits
of eagles, owls, vultures, and hawks.
  ISBN 0-8120-9424-7
  1. Birds of prey—Juvenile literature.   [1. Birds of prey.]
I. Title.
QL696.F3J8413   1996
598.9'1—dc20   95-47343
                                                              CIP
                                                              AC

Printed in Spain
6789 9960 987654321

J598.91
JUL
C1

DRIFTWOOD LIBRARY
OF LINCOLN CITY
801 S.W. Highway 101
Lincoln City, Oregon 97367

Penworthy   15⁴⁹   3-31-97

THE FASCINATING WORLD OF...

BIRDS OF PREY

by

Maria Ángels Julivert

Illustrations by Marcel Socías Studios

BARRON'S

MASTERS OF THE AIR

Like all birds, the bodies of birds of prey are covered in feathers. In addition to being useful for flying, feathers also allow them to keep their body temperature constant. For this reason they always have to keep their plumage in perfect condition. They have baths and clean their feathers carefully, and they waterproof them by impregnating them with the oil secreted by the **uropygial gland**, which is located at the base of the tail.

Although their plumage is beautiful, it is usually not very bright, combining shades of browns, blacks, and grays. The reason for these discreet colors is very simple: These birds are hunters and they need to go unnoticed by camouflaging themselves with their surroundings. They also have very sharp claws and a strong, hooked beak for immobilizing and catching their prey.

Birds of prey are divided into two large groups: diurnal and nocturnal. The former belong to the order **Falconiformes**. They hunt during the day, are very svelte in form, have very acute vision, and fly extremely fast.

The latter, in contrast, belonging to the order **Strigiformes**, have short, fat bodies, soft feathers, and but silent flight, with excepti hearing that allows them to h the lightest sounds, and sight

DIURNAL BIRD OF PREY

that is adapted to nocturnal vision.

NOCTURNAL BIRD OF PREY

Right: White-headed eagle washing its feathers.

CROWN

NOSTRILS

NAPE

BASAL CERA

WRIST

SCAPULAE

ALULAE

COVERTS

LEGS

TARSUS

RUMP

TALONS

PRIMARY REMIGES

RECTRICES

BUZZARD   VULTURE   FISH EAGLE

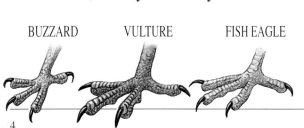

COURTSHIP FLIGHTS

During the mating season, each pair of birds occupies a **territory** that it defends from intruders, especially from other birds of the same species. Some birds of prey, however, like the Griffon vulture or the Eleonora's falcon, make nests in small groups. The breeding season is not the same for all species, but it always coincides with the time of year when conditions of **climate** and food are the most favorable for the bird.

During courtship, many birds of prey perform distinctive acrobatic flights, and often the male offers the female some prey as a present. Some perform an undulating flight, swooping and climbing again and again. Others fly very high and then fold their wings and plunge headlong before flying up just as it seems they are about to hit the ground.

Some birds of prey use the same nest year after year, mending it and enlarging it according to their needs.

Normally both the male and the female participate in building the nest. They are usually very solid constructions, sometimes very large, and are made with branches lined with moss, leaves, feathers, etc.

C

Right: Golden eagles building their nest on inaccessible rocks.

Above: Courtship flights in which the male pretends to attack the female, while she turns her back on him with her feet extended. Sometimes the male and the female actually touch claws.

Left: Birds of prey install their nests in the most diverse places: on the tops of trees, like this golden eagle (A); o[r] between rocks of cliffs; and even in old, abandoned buildings or on the ground, like the marsh harrier (B). There are also birds of prey, like the tawny owl (C), that do not construct their nests, but make use of natural cavities in trees and rocks, and there are even some that make use of nests abandoned by other birds.

A

B

REARING FLEDGLINGS

S ome birds of prey display sexual dimorphism, which means that the male and the female are different. The variations can be in size—in which case the female is usually larger than her partner—or in coloring.

Most birds of prey lay either two or three eggs, although some lay more than five or even, in the case of the black vulture, only one. The shape, size, and color of the eggs vary greatly. Although it is generally the female who sits on the eggs, among some birds of prey the male participates in this task.

The period of incubation, depending on the species, can last 23, 45, or even 60 days. As a general rule, it is longer for the large birds of prey, like the golden eagle and vultures. The chicks break the shell with the help of a tooth on the tip of the beak that they lose soon after being born. They are born covered with a fine, soft down. Feathers do not appear for a few weeks.

The young of birds of prey are **nidicolous**, which means that they are born defenseless and for a long time depend on their parents, who feed them by regurgitating food into their beaks. They do not leave the nest definitively for a long time. Young vultures are, without a doubt, the birds that stay in the nest for the longest time; they do not take their first flight until they are four months old.

A PAIR OF EAGLE OWLS

Right: For the initial days after hatching, one of the parents has to stay constantly in the nest while the other hunts. Also, while the young do not have their final feathers, the body of the mother or father protects them from the cold or heat.

A PAIR OF SPARROW-HAWKS

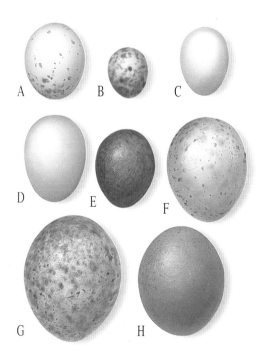

Left: Eggs of
A. Black kite,
B. Common kestrel
C. Barn owl
D. Goshawk,
E. Peregrine falcon
F. Golden eagle
G. Black vulture
H. Bearded eagle

PEREGRINE FALCON

EXPERT HUNTERS

Birds of prey are excellent hunters and feed on a wide variety of animals, which they swallow whole, although when the prey is too large, they tear it to pieces. The parts that they cannot digest—like the skin, feather, and bones—they regurgitate in the form of little balls called **pellets**. Their diet consists of mammals (mice, rabbits), other birds (partridges, doves, ducks), as well as reptiles (lizards), amphibians (frogs), and insects (grasshoppers, beetles); some even feed on fish or, like vultures, carrion.

Each bird of prey prefers a specific type of prey, of course. The fish eagle, for example, is called that because it eats fish almost exclusively. The short-toed eagle and the secretary bird prefer snakes, reptiles, and amphibians. For this reason, these birds have large feet that are covered with hard scales.

Other birds of prey, like the quick falcon or the swift kite, capture their prey in full flight. There are also those that catch their prey on the ground. They keep a constant watch from a branch or on a post or a rock, and when the opportunity arrives, they stealthily launch themselves

upon their prey. Finally there are other species, like the eagle or the vulture, that fly at a great height over their hunting territory, and others, like the kite or the harrier that prefer to fly almost touching the ground to explore their territory.

PELLETS

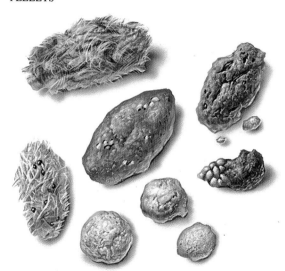

GOSHAWK

Right: The secretary bird is a very strange bird that lives on the planes and savannahs of Africa; it measures five feet (1$\frac{1}{2}$ meters) tall and is remarkable for its extraordinarily large feet. It has a strange crest of feathers on its head, the tips of its wings are black, and it has a splendid tail.

Above: A peregrine falcon hunts a bird in midair.

Left: Different types of pellets. By examining their contents it is possible to find out what food the bird has regurgitated.

Below: The sequence of attack of a goshawk.

DIURNAL BIRDS OF PREY

KITE BUZZARD GOSHAWK SPARROW HAWK

S ight is the most highly evolved sense in diurnal birds of prey. Their large, beady eyes allow them to notice the slightest movement among vegetation and to locate their prey even from a great height. Apart from some eagles and the bearded vulture, most have featherless tarsi and legs. Their feet have four toes, and so that they can grip, three of them point forward and the other one, backward.

The order of **Falconiforms** includes a large number of species spread over almost all the planet. Likewise, their appearance, size, and customs are varied. The condor, with a **wingspan** of 10 feet (3 meters), is one of the biggest, and some of the tiny African falcons, which are barely 6½ inches (14 centimeters) long, are among the smallest. The most numerous family is that of the *Accipitroidea* or **accipiters**, which includes, among others, the rapid sparrow hawks and kites, buzzards, eagles, kites, vultures, and harriers. The fish eagle forms a separate family. Falcons, kestrels, and hobbies belong to the family of the *Falconidae*. American vultures form the family of the *Cathartidae*.

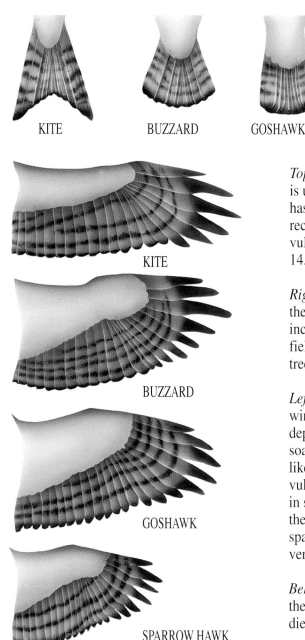

KITE

BUZZARD

GOSHAWK

SPARROW HAWK

Top: The tail, which is used as a rudder, has 12 feathers, called rectrices, except in vultures, which have 14.

Right: The habitat of the black-winged kite includes cultivated fields, meadows, and trees where it nests.

Left: The shape of the wings is varied. It depends whether they soar at great height, like eagles and vultures, or maneuver in sudden turns, like the goshawk and the sparrow hawk, or fly very fast, like falcons.

Below: The shape of the beak indicates the diet of each prey.

KITE BUZZARD GOSHAWK SPARROW HAW

THE FISH EAGLE

COMMON FISH EAGLE

This bird is called the fish eagle because it feeds almost exclusively on fish. The underside of its feet is covered with scales so that it can grip onto its slippery prey. Its claws are strong, sharp, and curved. This beautiful bird of prey always lives near rivers, lakes, or the coast; places near to water, either fresh or salt, which guarantee its supply of food.

From a high vantage point, or during slow flights, it watches the surface of the water and when it discovers some fish, it launches itself rapidly headlong at the prey with its wings folded. As it nears the surface, it opens its wings to brake its speed, extends its claws, and traps the fish. It rarely fails once it has chosen its prey.

It nests in trees or cliffs, and usually always uses the same nest, which it builds from a base of branches and then lines with grass, moss, or seaweed to make it more comfortable. It usually lays three eggs. The fish eagle can be found throughout most of the world, although in some areas its numbers have diminished and it is in danger of extinction.

Fish also form part of the diets of other birds of prey. Sea eagles of the genus **Haliaeetus**, like the white-tailed eagle, the African fish eagle, or the beautiful

white-headed American eagle, eat fish as well as sea birds and small mammals. The white-headed eagle is the symbol of America.

WHITE-HEADED EAGLE

WHITE-TAILED EAGLE

Right: An African fish eagle in the act of catching a fish.

Above: Sequence of fishing of a common fish eagle. It dives with its claws pointing forward to grip the fish. Once it is in the nest it will eat the fish in peace.

THE RAPID FALCON

They are fast and agile. Their long, narrow, pointed wings allow them to fly at great speed. They are falcons, from the family of the *Falconidae* and they prefer to eat other birds, which they hunt in flight, although some, like the lesser kestrel, prefer insects or even catch small mammals.

The falcon hardly ever builds its nest, but lays its eggs directly on rocks of a cliff or in nests abandoned by other birds. Some, like the lesser kestrel or Eleonora's falcon, make small colonies.

The gerfalcon is one of the largest (20–22 in. or 50–56 cm long). In winter it emigrates to warmer regions.

The peregrine falcon is possibly the most well known and also the most rapid of the birds of prey, capable of reaching 25 miles (200 kilometers) per hour when it dives on its prey, which it catches in mid flight. It feeds almost exclusively on other birds, such as ducks, pigeons, swifts, and seagulls.

There are other species of kestrel spread all over the world and in very different environments. In the United States the American kestrel is very common, while in Europe and Africa the most common are the common kestrel and the lesser kestrel, respectively. The males of these two species have a gray-blue colored head and tail. Unlike most birds of prey, whose claws are black, the lesser kestrel's claws are white.

PEREGRINE FALCON

HOBBY

PIGEON HAWK

Above: The hobby is barely 14 inches (35 cm) long. Even smaller is the pigeon hawk, which is between 11 and 13 inches (27 and 33 cm) long.

Right: The common kestrel carries its prey to a vantage point to eat it, while it keeps a watch on its surroundings.

ELEONORA'S FALCON

AMERICAN KESTREL

801 S.W. Highway 101
Lincoln City, Oregon 97367

THE MAJESTIC EAGLE

Eagles have legs covered with feathers down to the feet. Like vultures, these birds of prey soar to great heights by using rising currents of air. They build their nests on the peaks of trees or on rocky cliffs, making platforms of branches, which they cover with grass and moss. They usually use the same nest for several years.

Among birds of prey, the eagle is the most majestic. The golden eagle is one of the largest, measuring from 30 to 35 inches (75 to 88 centimeters) in length. It is dark brown in color, and the tips of its wings are black. The imperial eagle is a little smaller, has darker plumage, and prefers to make its nest in trees.

But not all eagles are so large; the booted eagle measures between 18 and 21 inches (45 and 53 centimeters) and its flight is one of the fastest. Always aggressive, the small Bonelli's eagle will not hesitate to attack with fury any intruder that comes close to its nest clinging to a rocky cliff.

Eagles belong to the large *Accipitroidea* family, like the harrier that lives in the marshy wetland regions of Asia, Africa, Australia, and America. They make their nests on the ground, camouflaged between the vegetation. Others, like the buzzards, are also very skilled at soaring, though at a lower height than eagles and vultures. Kites are found in a multitude of habitats, thanks to their ability to modify their diet and even to feed on carrion, as vultures do. As for sparrow hawks and goshawks, these are birds that can fly very fast and with great agility.

SPARROW HAWK

MARSH HARRIER

Right: This magnificent bird of prey, the golden eagle, lives in mountainous regions and builds its nest on high crags.

BONELLI'S EAGLE

GOSHAWK

BOOTED EAGLE

BLACK KITE

THE VULTURE, A GLIDER

GRIFFON VULTURE

CONDOR

KING VULTURE

BLACK VULTURE

True to its reputation, the vulture feeds on **carrion** and waste. To locate dead animals, it uses its acute vision and excellent sense of smell. It makes use of currents of warm air to rise in the sky until it reaches a great height, and then it slowly glides downward. Most vultures join together in groups that are often very numerous. Others, like the black vulture and the condor, prefer solitude or life in pairs. Sometimes a vulture eats so much food that it is unable to take off again until some time has passed.

Vultures' heads and necks are bare and have no feathers except for a beautiful collar of very fine white feathers around their necks. There are different species of vultures, which are divided into two families. The *Accipitroidea* live in Europe, Asia, and Africa. The black vulture, the griffon vulture, and the Egyptian vulture belong to this group. On the other hand there are the American vultures of the *Cathartidae* family; these include the black vulture, the turkey vulture, the distinctive king vulture, and the great condor.

The Andean condor is one of the largest birds that exists, with a **wingspan** of up to 10 feet (3 meters) long and doubtless is the one that can fly the highest. The males sport a large crest on their heads and under their beaks is a single fold of skin. The king vulture is a very distinctive bird of prey thanks to its head, which is brightly colored with yellow, orange, and red. Its plumage is black and white. Other smaller birds of prey, like the black vulture, move away and leave them space at the carrion when they approach.

Right: A group of vultures eating their prey. The griffon vulture is a large bird of prey, with brown plumage and a white collar. The black vulture is even larger, with a dark collar and plumage.

THE BEARDED VULTURE AND THE EGYPTIAN VULTURE

The bearded vulture is a large bird of prey with an elegant form and distinctive plumage. Its wings and tail are dark in contrast to its breast, which is a reddish-orange color. From its beak hangs a tuft of bristle that gives it a very strange appearance. The bearded vulture lives in mountainous regions and nests in high crags, where it constructs large platforms out of branches. It feeds on dead animals and one of its favorite foods is bone marrow. When the bones are large and cannot be split open, it drops them onto rocks from a great height so that they break.

The Egyptian vulture is a small bird of prey, some 28 inches (70 centimeters) long and weighing 4½ pounds (2 kilograms). Its plumage is whitish, its face yellow, and its beak long and fine. It lives in Europe, Asia, and Africa. It feeds on carrion and waste; it can also catch small vertebrates and mammals and it loves eggs. To break them it drops them on the ground, but if they are very large, it uses a tool. To break the shell of an enormous ostrich egg, the Egyptian vulture takes a stone and drops it on the egg as often as needed to break it.

Right and below: The Egyptian vulture is one of the few animals that uses tools. It picks up a stone, raises it, and drops it on the egg. If it does not manage to break it, it repeats the operation.

Left: The plumage of the young Egyptian vulture is brown.

Above: The Egyptian vulture is an easy bird to recognize because of its yellow head and white plumage.

Left: A brown fringe surrounds the eyes of thc bearded vulture and a tuft of bristles clings to its beak.

NOCTURNAL HUNTERS

Nocturnal birds of prey belong to the order of **Strigiformes**. They have large, round heads, with big eyes pointing forward marked by a circle of feathers. Their legs are covered with feathers and often so are their toes, of which two point forward and two backward.

One strange thing about these birds is that their ears are arranged asymmetrically, one higher than the other. The **Strigiformes** hunt by night and rest by day. They stay by the trunk of a tree, and thanks to the coloration of their plumage, they remain invisible.

Nocturnal birds of prey form two families: the *Tytonidae,* a small family that includes the well-known barn owl, and the *Strigidae,* which includes the rest.

The barn owl has beautiful, golden plumage that is complemented by a pattern of gray marks in the upper part of its body and white ones in the lower part. Its disc of facial feathers is in the shape of a heart. The barn owl frequents cultivated regions and open spaces. Its favorite food is rodents, although it also likes to catch other birds, amphibians, and insects.

Above: Nocturnal birds of prey can turn their heads almost 180° in each direction.

Right: The barn owl hunts rodents, which it gives whole to its young.

Left: The tawny owl spends the night waiting patiently camouflaged in the hollow of a tree.

Below: A map of the distribution of nocturnal birds of prey.

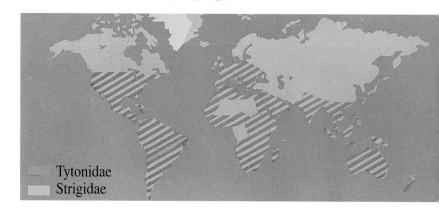

Tytonidae
Strigidae

EAGLE OWLS AND FAMILY

The second family of nocturnal birds of prey, the *Strigidae* are much more numerous. These include, among others, eagle owls, little owls, short-eared owls, tawny owls, and scops owls. Some species are very similar and it is easy to confuse them. Others, in contrast, are easy to recognize, such as the great grey owl or the snowy owl. In reality there are many details that can help to identify them, from the color of the eyes to the size of the body.

The eyes of the tawny owl are black, of the scops owl, yellow, and of the eagle owl, orange. Some species, like the scops owl, the eagle owl, and the long-eared owl, have a tuft of feathers on their heads that they raise or flatten according to their state of mind. The tawny owl and the short-eared owl do not have a crest like this, while in the barn owl it is so small that it can hardly be seen.

The biggest species of this family are the eagle owl, the snowy owl, and the Virginia owl. Among the smallest are the scops owl, the elf owl, and the pygmy owl. Most *Strigidae* come out to hunt for food at dusk, but there are also some that hunt during the day, like the hawk owl and the squat common little owl.

LONG-EARED OWL

TAWNY OWL

GREAT GREY OWL

SHORT-EARED OWL

SCOPS OWL

LITTLE OWL

SNOWY OWL

Right: The eagle owl comes out to hunt at dawn and dusk. It is an expert hunter that traps small mammals, reptiles, and amphibians as well as other birds, including birds of prey such as kestrels, buzzards, scops owls, and tawny owls.

Below: The snowy owl lives in the arctic tundra. The males have beautiful, immaculate white plumage, while the females are dotted with dark marks. When winter comes, some snowy owls migrate south looking for areas where they can find food.

HUMANS, THEIR GREATEST THREAT

Adult birds of prey do not have a great number of natural enemies other than some mammals, reptiles, and other birds. The young and the eggs, on the other hand, are much more vulnerable.

However, as so often is the case, humans are the greatest enemy of these beautiful birds. Many have been persecuted for killing domestic animals or catching other birds that man hunts. Even so, birds of prey are more beneficial than they are harmful. Most species, both **nocturnal** and **diurnal**, devour an enormous number of rodents that damage human crops. Carrion eaters also carry out an important role in natural balance by feeding on dead animals that could spread infections if left to rot.

Despite this, humans continue to put these beautiful birds in danger, by hunting them illegally, destroying their natural habitats, or polluting the environment. Toxic substances from pesticides accumulate in the bodies of these birds, causing death or alterations in their eggs, such as shells that are much softer and easy to break. Intrusion into their nesting areas is also a major factor, since if they are disturbed they might abandon the nest.

The black vulture, the golden eagle, the bearded eagle, and many other birds of prey are in serious danger of extinction.

Above: Toxic substances from pesticides accumulate as they climb up the food chain. Birds of prey are at the top of the chain.

Right: When they feel threatened, birds of prey try to simulate a larger size by fluffing up their plumage, extending their wings, and even making the feathers on their heads and necks stand on end.

Left: With the disappearance of vegetation, birds of prey cannot survive.

Below: Combine harvesters destroy the brood of the Montagu's harrier.

Left: Illegal hunting is another cause for worry.

GLOSSARY

Accipitroidea: Family of diurnal birds of prey of the order of Falconiformes.

carrion: Dead animals on which some birds feed.

Cathartidae: Family of diurnal birds of prey that include the American vulture.

colony: Group of animals of the same species that live in the same territory.

Falconidae: Family of diurnal birds of prey of the order Falconiformes that includes falcons.

Falconiformes: Order of birds that includes diurnal birds of prey, such as falcons, kites, vultures, and eagles, among others.

food chain: Scheme of food relationships by level. Species in the top line are predators of the line below and so on.

nidicolous: Birds whose young are born defenseless and unable to feed themselves and who stay in the nest for a certain time being looked after by the parents.

pellet: Remains of undigested food regurgitated by some birds.

rectrices: Feathers of a bird's tail.

regurgitate: Return food to the mouth from the esophagous or the stomach without digesting it.

Strigidae: Family of nocturnal birds of prey of the order of Strigiformes that includes eagle owls.

territory: Specific area or place occupied by an animal, which it will defend from other animals of the same species.

Tytonidae: Small family of birds of prey that includes the barn owl.

uropygial gland: A secretor organ located at the base of the tail of many birds.

wingspan: Distance between the tips of the wings when they are completely open. In contrast to the length of a bird, which is measured between the head and the point of the feet.

INDEX

DRIFTWOOD LIBRARY
OF LINCOLN CITY
801 S.W. Highway 101
Lincoln City, Oregon 97367